D1605466

THE BLACKBIRD'S NEST

Saint Kevin of Ireland

written by Jenny Schroedel & illustrated by Doug Montross

ST VLADIMIR'S SEMINARY PRESS ✦ YONKERS ✦ NEW YORK

arly one morning, when all of Ireland slept beneath a quilt of wintry white, a baby boy was born. His mother traced his wrinkle of a mouth, his perfect eyelashes and half-moon fingernails. She kissed his forehead, as warm and soft as bread dough.

As she cradled her babe at the open door, her eyes widened with wonder. In the forest beyond, snowflakes coated the tree branches, but melted the moment they touched the earth encircling her home. She had never seen such a thing before.

When the baby was forty days old, he was baptized. As the priest lifted the infant from the water, he blessed him and said, "Beautiful child of God, you shall be called Kevin, meaning *gentle one.*"

But the gentle baby Kevin grew into a mischievous boy. He chased girls with stinging nettles and shoved smaller boys out of his way. When the village children saw him coming, they ducked into their homes. He pushed. He shoved. He bullied. He was anything but gentle.

But with animals, Kevin was different. When they heard his footsteps in the woods, they waited. Deer stood still so he could pet them; butterflies lit on his shoulders; and geese followed him home. Kevin befriended every animal he met.

This puzzled his parents. Their son was so awkward with people, yet completely at home with animals.

When the front door creaked open, they cringed. What creature was Kevin clutching this time? Was it an injured goose, a snapping turtle, or a scrawny puppy? At night Kevin shared his bed with his animal friends, whose soft breathing lulled him to sleep.

When he was seven, Kevin's parents sent him to live at a monastery where he could learn to read, write, and pray. As he knelt beside the monks in chapel, he felt he almost belonged there.

But the monks struggled with unruly Kevin. He tripped over their feet when he rushed late into chapel; he pretended not to hear when they reminded him to scrub the hallway floors; and sometimes he even snuck into the kitchen and stole bread for the ducks.

As Kevin grew older, the monks only grew wearier of his antics. One year, when he was a teenager, they asked him to spend the forty days of Lent praying alone in a desolate valley. As he trudged to his solitary hut, he wondered why no one wanted him around. He felt very alone.

The next morning, while Kevin prayed with his arms outstretched through the window of his hut, he felt something drop into his hand. He opened his eyes. A blackbird perched on his open palm with a twig in her beak. She looked directly at Kevin, as if to ask a question.

Over the next few days, Kevin held out his arm as the blackbird wove a nest of stalks, moss, and twigs in his hand. Kevin cradled the nest even as the blackbird laid her eggs. "Lord have mercy," he whispered.

Day followed day, and Kevin stood as still as a tree. He ate the berries the blackbird fed him and drank the dew on his lips. He did not even scratch his nose, although he desperately wanted to. His knees were stiff; his outstretched arm was growing weak; and his fingers were turning blue. "Lord have mercy," he whispered.

One morning, Kevin awoke to a wiggling egg. Days later, the egg split open, revealing a scrawny, exhausted chick. A second egg wiggled. Within a few days the nest was full of newly hatched chicks. "Lord have mercy," Kevin whispered.

Soon the fast-growing chicks peered over the nest's rim. Kevin watched as the baby birds learned to fly—they flexed their oversized wings, flopped from the nest, and landed in the dirt.

Forty days after the mother blackbird first lit on Kevin's hand, the last baby bird left the nest. Kevin collapsed on the flagstone floor of his hut, closed his eyes, and whispered, "Amen."

Kevin slept for hours. When he awoke, his body ached. Suddenly the words from his baptism came to him: "Beautiful child of God. You shall be called Kevin, meaning *gentle one*."

He knew that it was time to let people—not just animals—into his heart. He leapt to his feet. He must return to the monastery for the great feast of Christ's Resurrection.

Kevin arrived just in time. During the service, candlelight spread from one wick to the next, and brightness surged through Kevin's soul. Holding his own flickering candle, he peered into the faces of his brother monks. It was as if he was seeing them for the very first time.

Kevin never forgot the spring the blackbirds hatched in his hand. One day he returned to the valley where he spent that long ago Lent and founded a new monastery.

Kevin lived to be one hundred twenty years old and took his last breath encircled by his beloved fellow monks. He was buried near the monastery church. For more than a thousand years, pilgrims have flocked there to pray. But years of wind, rain, snow, and sunshine have worn the words off the gravestones, and nobody is quite sure where his body lies.

But the blackbirds remember. When the din of the pilgrims' voices and footsteps fade away, they return. Perching on a single weathered cross, they sing gently to their friend.

Historical Note

Saint Kevin was born in Ireland in AD 498 to a royal family. According to legend, his mother gave birth to him without pain or struggle. The first winter of Kevin's life, the snow that fell on his home melted, as if a circle of warmth protected the house. He was baptized by Saint Cronan and given the name Coemgen, or *Kevin*, meaning *of fair birth*, or *gentle one*.

When Kevin was seven years old, his parents sent him to be educated at a monastery, where he studied under Saint Petroc of Cornwall. After he was ordained to the priesthood, he lived as a hermit for seven years. He eventually became the abbot and founder of Glendalough, one of Ireland's most famous monasteries. Just before he died in AD 618, he visited with Saint Ciaran. Saint Kevin's feast day is commemorated on third of June.

Hymn to Saint Kevin

TROPARION

Saint Kevin's life was first recorded 400 years after his death. Therefore, many of the accounts of his life are fragmentary and legendary. Sources suggest that Saint Kevin was a quirky fellow, struggling with other people but at ease with wild creatures and his Creator. Saint Kevin's life was enriched by his friendship with winged and four-legged creatures; he remains as an example of ceaseless prayer and brave gentleness.

Bird experts have observed that the nesting process for blackbirds can take as long as forty days, from the first nesting twig to the last fledgling's flight. So, too, the season of Lent is forty days long. Just as Kevin waited for the baby birds to break open their eggs and come to new life in his hand, during Lent we wait for Christ to break open the tomb and bring new life into our hearts.

You were privileged to live in the age of saints, O Father Kevin, being baptized by one saint, taught by another, and buried by a third. Pray to God that he will raise up saints in our day to help, support, and guide us in the way of salvation.

To my father, for his infinite patience with winged creatures.

The author also wishes to gratefully acknowledge the following word experts, bird experts, and friends of Saint Kevin: Jim Manolis, David Stein, Father Kevin Scherer, Nicholas Groves, Richard Marsh, Amber Schley, Anne Hopko, and Mary Gregory.

— J. S.

To Stephen, Caitlin, Mackensie, Courtlandt, Hayden, and Garrett.

— D. M.

The publication of this book was made possible by a generous gift from Mark and Hresula Hudoff, in honor of their son Frederick and in memory of their grandparents, Ruth and Tolmie and Nick and Eleni, who devoted their lives to tilling God's earth and who rejoiced in the wonder of His creation.

LIBRARY OF CONGRESS CATALOGING-IN-PUBLICATION DATA

Schroedel, Jenny.
    The blackbird's nest : Saint Kevin of Ireland / Jenny Schroedel; illustrated by Doug Montross.
      p. cm.
    ISBN 0-88141-258-9
    1. Kevin, Saint, Abbot of Glendalough, d. 618—Juvenile literature.
    2. Christian saints—Ireland—Glendalough—Biography—Juvenile literature.
    I. Montross, Doug. II. Title.

    BX4700.K4S37 2004
    270.2'092—DC22
    [B]   2004041759

ST VLADIMIR'S SEMINARY PRESS
575 Scarsdale Road • Yonkers • New York • 10707-1699
1-800-204-BOOK
www.svspress.com

ISBN 978-0-88141-258-1

First printed in 2004, reprinted in 2015

Text copyright © 2004 Jenny Schroedel
Illustrations copyright © 2004 Doug Montross

Icon of St Kevin used by kind permission of St Kevin's Parish, Glendalough, Co. Wicklow, Ireland

Book and cover design: Amber Schley

All Rights Reserved. No part of this book may be reproduced or transmitted in any form or by any means, electronic or mechanical, including photocopying, recording, or by any information storage or retrieval system, without prior permission in writing from the publisher.

PRINTED IN CHINA